Operating Holistic Enterprise

Tips of the Trade

By
Charles Lightwalker

MAPLE
PUBLISHERS

Operating a Holistic Enterprise Tips of the Trade

Author: Charles Lightwalker

First Published in 2024

ISBN 978-1-83538-198-4 (Paperback)

Published by:

Maple Publishers
Fairbourne Drive, Atterbury,
Milton Keynes,
MK10 9RG, UK
www.maplepublishers.com

Table of Contents

Authors Page

This book is an outgrowth of my workshops on operating a holistic enterprise.

After many years as an Intuitive Business Counselor, counseling hundreds of business enterprises, I have come to the realization that a manual was necessary for the holistic practitioner.

Most holistic minded people get into their business to serve humanity, to help people on their path to wholeness, to wellness, to understanding what they need to maintain balance, harmony and health in their life.

I have been guided on this great journey of mine to be of service to those that need guidance, healing, and self-empowerment.

I would like to thank those that have helped me on this part of my journey of Intuitive business counseling; Ben Cabildo of ANANA, his wisdom has been of great help in understanding my role in the process of helping serve the holistic community and in forming the holistic chamber of commerce.

To Harvey Cain a friend, racquetball/tennis partner, he has given me the male perspective of the holistic business world, as he is one of the finest massage therapists I have ever known. To Bob King a dear friend a fellow holistic practitioner, for his wisdom and insight into the business of operating a partnership business with others. To Pam Albee who operates Shared Transitions, to Debra Eaglewoman an incredible shaman and friend. To Serena LaSol my partner, wife, confidant and mother to our daughter Mayah. To Mayah LaSol for being the daughter that always reminds me that I am just Daddy, and keep me grounded. To all my apprentices who have crossed my path and have given to me so many wonderful experiences.

And to my Dad Eddie for his insight, love and wisdom.

This book is dedicated to all those who seek to serve the human race into seeking the highest good for all.

Charles Lightwalker, 2007

Chapter 1

A Holistic Enterprise

Operating a holistic business is really no different from any other business in that you need to follow many of the same business rules such as keeping books, advertising, renting office space, having products or services to offer.

How a holistic enterprises differs is that most practitioners get into this business because they care, they want to help people and have a holistic mind set that see the world from a different perspective than the normal business owner, they see the world as a sacred place from which all of life

Is nourished from the integrative process of interaction.

In the following chapters I will discuss the process of operating a holistic enterprise. Why one must follow the rules of managing a business such as bookkeeping, advertising, having a business plan and goals.

I have operated several businesses in my life, from retail to service, and currently serve as Director of the Family of Light Healing Centre, an international mobile healing and educational centre.

Success is not in the business being huge or making a lot of money, but in the pleasure you get from feeling that you are operating a business, which feeds your soul and pays the bills.

That doesn't mean that you cannot make a lot of money but that is not the main objective, it is a bi-product of the dedication and hard work you put into the operation of your holistic business.

In these book I will give you tips on how to operate the most successful business you can, I will share with you the successes and failures I have made on my journey into the holistic arena.

Chapter 2

Business Plan- Ideas for the Holistic Practitioner

A business plan communicates your businesses direction.
It should be clear, straight forward and to the point.

Components of a typical business plan:

Summary:
This is a short summarization of your whole plan. Put best business face forward in a complete and concise manner. It serves as quick reference and read for everyone from, your employees, bankers or investors. This is also the place to discuss how much funding you are requesting, what you will use the funds for, and a plan of how to pay back investors.

Vision of Your business, an Overview:
Describe your business, your target market, goals and objectives. Give an overall view of your growth strategies. How are you different from your competitors?

Products and Services:
Describe what your services (or products), including fee's charged, prices of products, quality of products/services and your unique selling proposition.

Market Analysis:
Analysis of your market and client/customer base. Identity of your clientele/customers –

Demographically and psycho graphically, characteristics of your industry and opportunities with regards to market entry.

Competitive Analysis:
Examines your major competition. Develops comparison between your strength and weakness. Identifies how you differentiate yourself from the competition. List your competitive advantages.

Marketing and Sales:
Describe your overall marketing strategies and tactics. Outlines your plan of positioning your business in the holistic marketplace, attracting and retaining clients/customers.

Management and Organization:
Describe your management experience.

Financials:
Includes balance sheet Projection (assets, liabilities and owner's equity.
12 month profit projection.
Cash flow projection for next 3 years.

A Business Plan Serves Two Functions:

Firstly, it can be presented to a bank or another investor to explain to them what it is you plan to do, and how you plan to go about it. Anyone lending money to someone starting a business venture will want to see evidence of market research and financial planning before they write out a check.

Secondly, it is a good way of organizing your thoughts, thereby making sure you don't miss anything. The process of writing a business plan will make you aware of any shortcomings in your preparations, and will give you a chance to rectify the situation before launching your venture.

Put simply, it is the blueprint from which you will work, allowing you to methodically carry out the tasks needed to make your practice a success.

A healthcare practice is no different from any other business venture when formulating a business plan. There is never an absolute guarantee how a business will develop with the fullness of time; however, good advice in the beginning usually avoids problems later.

Most local banks or independent business advisors should be in a position to give professional advice on the matter. This article is in no way intended as a substitute for this kind of one-on-one business consultation. Every venture will have its own unique character, so it is advisable to seek professional advice.

What this article will do is provide a guide to what a professional business advisor will be looking for in a good business plan. Use it as you start to put down your ideas on paper, and then seek professional advice about your individual circumstances. Having something down in writing to begin with will look more professional than going to a meeting with only a vague notion of what you want to do.

The First Thing An Investor Will Look For

Most business advisors/investors will turn straight to the back when handed a business plan - traditionally, this is where the cash-flow projections will be.

A simple chart, divided into monthly columns, showing what your expected incomings and outgoings will be, with a net total at the bottom.

Put simply, this lets an investor (and you!) know if your practice is going to be viable or not. Few businesses turn a profit within the first six months of trading - any money taken will cover start-up costs, and will generally be re-invested to help the business grow.

But if the business is making huge losses for the first year or more, with no profits in sight on the horizon, few people will consider it a worthwhile venture. Certainly, such a business will have a hard time finding investors outside of eccentric millionaire philanthropists!

So, in a sense, it can be worthwhile to start at the back and work forwards. Everything else in your business plan will be there to explain the figures in your cash flow projections.

If the figures look good, you'll have caught a potential investor's attention - then, he/she will want to know how you arrived at them.

A Simple Cash Flow Forecast

Open a spreadsheet program, or take a piece of paper. Divide it into 15 separate columns.

These will be a title cell (what the expense/source of income will be); pre-start up costs/investments; the twelve months of your first year of trading (depending on when you launch); and a grand total column.

Then, starting at the top, draw up as many rows as you need for all your incomings, with a total underneath for each month, and underneath those, all your expenses, with another total. The bottom row on your page will be your net profit for each month - the total figure of all your incomings minus your outgoings.

Then, the final cell, in the bottom right hand corner of your page will be your total profit or loss for the year.

As a therapist, your incomings will be simple - estimate how many clients you hope to see each month, and multiply that by your consultation fee.

Your outgoings will be a little more complicated, and it may appear daunting at first as you start to list all the things you'll be paying out for! There are always so many more little expenses (and not so little ones!) that you suddenly think of when you sit down to work it out.

Depending on whether you are working from home or renting premises there will be your rent; utility bills; various professional insurances; various promotional costs (brochures, website hosting; print ads). Not to mention all the administration costs that soon mount up like telephone bills, office supplies, etc.

Start with rough estimates, to keep things simple. As you do more research in the course of writing you business plan, you'll be able to provide more accurate figures.

Providing Evidence To Explain Your Cash Flow Projections

Once you're happy with the basic layout of your cash flow chart, you have to provide the evidence that will explain how you arrived at certain figures.
The rest of your business plan will be broken down into the following sub-sections:

Business Description

This should be a short description of yourself and what you intend to do. Don't be afraid to write down everything, as it is better to state the obvious than to be ambiguous in a business plan. Assume that your reader knows nothing about healthcare at all, and explain exactly what you intend to do.

Market Research

It is no good to just say `I'm going to start up an acupuncture clinic' and leave it at that. Certainly, there are thousands of very profitable acupuncture clinics, but it is here that you really need to convince someone else that there is a demand for what you propose to do. This is where you need to provide hard facts and figures to explain the cash flow projections you've provided at the end of your business plan.

Include statistics relating to the alternative healthcare profession. Describe the type of person you expect to be treating. There's no such thing as an `average person' of course, but you need to give a rough indication of your target market and `ideal customer'.

Investors will also want to see evidence of Direct & Indirect Competition

Are you starting an acupuncture clinic in a large town with no other acupuncturists in practice? If so, you have no Direct Competition, and are in a very strong position business-wise.

If, however, you are starting a clinic in a tiny village with only 600 occupants, and there's an acupuncturist who's been in practice for twenty years, you might have your work cut out trying to find clients!

Indirect Competition can be anything from another therapist in your field in a neighboring town (particularly if he/she has a good reputation and people are prepared to travel); or other therapists in similar fields (some health problems will respond to different therapies).

It is perhaps less relevant to healthcare - people will tend to put their health before other things - but Indirect Competition can be anything that is competing for peoples' disposable income, such as entertainment, travel, etc.

Whatever your individual circumstances are, investors will want to see evidence that you are aware of these factors.

To summarize: You need to provide evidence there is a demand for the service you propose to provide; whom that demand will be from; how many of these people you can potentially attract (remembering that, as a therapist, your catchments area will be limited); and how much you will be charging these people, based on the fees of other therapists.

Promotion

Investors will also want to see details of the kind of promotion you intend to give your business. There's an old saying - `If you don't promote, something terrible happens - NOTHING!'

You'll want to demonstrate that you have a good grasp of the fundamentals of promotion, like your USP (Unique Selling Point).

What is your Unique Selling Point?

If you're the only person offering your therapy in a given area, it's obvious. But if you're intending to set up in practice in an area where there is some competition, you need to explain why it is people would seek treatment from you instead of someone else.

Certainly, a big city will be able to provide more than one acupuncturist with clients - but you need to give some reason why you feel people would be prepared to choose you over another therapist.

It might be something as simple as the convenient parking outside your proposed place of business. In a crowded city with zealous traffic wardens, this can be a big bonus for you!

Explanation Of Your Financial Plan

Once you have covered the more general aspects of your business, you will want to go into detail about the various items on your cash flow charts, and how you arrived at those figures.

How much are you charging clients, and why?

What is the average for your type of service?

Is the location of your business a factor?

Certainly, a therapist working in Beverly Hills will be charging more than a therapist working downtown - not only will his/her overheads be higher, but his/her patients will, in general, have more disposable income!

Evidence can also be provided here for your outgoings - rents, quotes from insurance companies, etc.

You'll want to provide three different scenarios: a best-case scenario, a worst-case scenario, and one somewhere in the middle.

It is always best to err on the side of caution. Don't be afraid to provide a pessimistic scenario - it proves to a potential investor that you are a realist, who doesn't expect to be able to retire within two years!

You may also find that even a worst-case scenario isn't as bad as you may have feared.

If you still start to show a modest profit eventually, an investor will be confident that your venture isn't a `money-pit' - that there will be a small return on their investment at some point.

In summary, your business plan should contain:

- Business Description
Who you are; what you intend to do; what you hope to achieve.

- Market Research
Who are your clients going to be? How many of them are there? Do you have any Direct/Indirect Competition?

- Promotion
What is your USP? How do you intend to let people know you're out there?

- Cash Flow Explanation
Explanations of the figures in your cash flow projections - your incomings and outgoings, how much they are going to be and why.

- Cash Flow Projections
Profit and Loss charts for at least the first 12 months of trading (preferably up to three years). Best, Worst, and Medium case scenarios.

Once you have these elements in place, you should seek a consultation with a small business advisor. They will be able to point out any shortcomings in your business plan.

Remember, your business plan is the blueprint for your practice. Whilst there are never any guarantees in business, a poor business plan will almost certainly result in problems down the line.

Chapter 3

Designing Your Brochures

Writing and designing a brochure for your business is an important step toward marketing yourself. Part of a successful marketing campaign includes written promotional materials: business cards, brochures, press kit, and fliers but we often get overwhelm when it comes to designing and making them. In my years as an intuitive business counselor to the holistic business community, I have found this is one of the most Difficult tasks for Holistic business owners to get completed. Holistic business owners are often intimidated by the writing and confused by all the design choices. By doing a little market research, organizing your thoughts, designing the space on paper, printing, and so forth, you can easily have a finished brochure within just a day or two.

Here are the steps I teach everyday as an intuitive business counselor.

First, collect business cards, brochures and fliers from other Holistic business owners. Acquire everything including the brochures that you like and ones that you do not like. Lay all these items in front of you on a large table. Then quickly, at first glance, put them into two piles. In one pile put all the brochures that you like, and in the other pile put the ones that you don't like. Do this quickly, without thinking too much. Rely on your intuition.

> **What do you notice about the ones you like?**
> **Is it the material?**
> **Color?**
> **Font?**

Repeat this process and do the same analysis of the materials that do not appeal to you. Make a few notes about your likes and dislikes. Toss your dislike pile out. Return to the appealing pile.

Pull out a few of your favorites and read them. Analyze your favorites in more detail and see if you can discover why you like them. Is it a simple design, full bright color, or a certain layout that appeals to you?
Do you like the feel of the paper or photos that are included? Is there a particular card or brochure that would prompt you to call and follow up with this person? What is it that makes you want to respond to the brochure? Take a few more notes about the things you like, be as specific as possible.

Now its time to think about what you would like in your brochure. Keep in mind this should be an invitation for a prospective client to phone you. You want maximum impact in a small space.

- What do you want on the front of the brochure?

- What is the first thing you want others to notice about you and your practice?

- Your face or other image?

- Will you include any photos at all?

- Will they be on the front or back of the brochure?

- Do you have a catchy name for your business?

- What is the most important thing about yourself that you want to include?

Clearly think through your features and benefits:

A brochure should clearly reflect who you are as a person and what your strengths are.

Your features include your training, location, skills, and professional associations you belong to.

Ask yourself:

- Why does the client care what type of training you have?

- How will it help them?

- Will it save them money?

- Make them feel better?

Take some time now to clearly think about your features and benefits. Write down everything about yourself that is marketable, everything you are proud of, and all your education. Now, translate all these features to benefits for your clients.

<u>Now its time for the writing</u>.

By following this simple template below, you will be able to write your promotional material with ease.

As you write your brochure keep it in clear concise language, free of industry jargon.
Keep in mind that the brochure will speak for you and should reflect your inner voice.
It can educate potential clients and ask them to contact you.

When writing the text of your brochure, ask the following questions:

Who? What? When? Where? Why? How? Write a little on each of the following questions.

Who am I and what are my credentials?
Who is my client- my audience?
What do I do? This is my feature.
What will the client get? This is the benefit.
When should they come?
When they hurt?
Or every month for maintenance?
When are you open?
Your hours and days of operation.
Why are you a practitioner?
What got you started?
What is your Why should a client come?
More benefits to them.
How do they make an appointment?

<u>Now,</u> take each answer and edit it down to one or two short simple sentences that clearly answer each question. Take these notes and lay them out on a plain piece of white paper, so you can start to look and feel how they will be laid out. You can also do this on your computer.

Finish with a call to action.

The prospective client should read your brochure and be motivated to call you.

Ask them to do something that inspires them to act, to call now, to mail in something, or to book an appointment.

Remember to ask them to do it, so they are left with an action step to take.

Go to the local office supply store and look through the stock selection of brochure papers.

Bring your notes with your likes and dislikes from your market research.
You will find that you can choose from several very pleasant low cost designs.

Find a simple design with lots of white space that you like. Consider a pretty 81/2 x 11 paper and fold it in half or thirds. When you have chosen, purchase the minimum amount to take home.

Lay it all out on the page.

Type all your text into the computer and then print it out on plain white paper. Cut it up into sections, and again lay it out on different places on the page. See what works and what don't. When you like the look of your layout, change it on the computer and print it out on your paper. Here are a few simple rules to keep in mind when designing a brochure.

Leave lots of white space. Don't fill the paper with too much text, as it can be difficult to read.

Choose one or two font types only. Keep the type size consistent. Include testimonials from others. Include your features and benefits. Have your contact information complete. Always include your area code.

Read and Re-read

Have a trusted friend; proofread all your written materials before printing your brochure. Print two brochures, one for yourself and one for another friend. Live with it overnight and see if there are any more changes before printing.

Now you are ready to print

Print only a minimum amount of brochures, maybe ten or so, and try them out before stocking up. 12. Its time to pass out your brochures everywhere. Your brochure will be many places at once, doing the marketing for you so we want to make sure that it stands out. Post your brochure on bulletin boards, in offices, and in waiting rooms to get your name out there. Your goal should be to have your name familiar to others in the community so that they easily recognize you and your brochure the second time they see it. In time, your prospective clients will have seen your name so much that they will feel as though they already know you.

Chapter 4

Attracting Clients

As a holistic healer it can be difficult to face the challenge of marketing yourself and building a clientele. This challenge can be enhanced by the desire not to commercialize holistic healing in compromise of your spiritual values. But holistic healers do not need to fear the process of building a successful practice, if the methods used to build them are honest, sincere and you have integrity.

A potential barrier to success that many holistic healers face in marketing themselves is the balance between the desire to give and the practicalities of living in an economically driven world. Often, a fear of receiving money for doing holistic healing interferes with the ability to build a thriving practice.

Earning money is not a bad thing - but possessing a belief that it is can sabotage your success in building a successful practice. One way to address this is to realize that what we get paid for our services as a holistic healer is an exchange of energy that recognizes the value of your healing knowledge and treatment process. By viewing money as a method of exchange that provides balance between client and healer we become more comfortable with our self worth and receiving financial abundance.

The techniques used in building any business can be used by the holistic practitioner, perhaps with a few minor adjustments and focusing on the intention behind them. The holistic healer must be clear in their mind that the purpose behind using marketing tools is to share their knowledge of holistic healing and living with the community, and then a successful relationship with clients can be reached.

One of the basic techniques for building any business is getting to know your clients. As a holistic healer your clients are those who come to you to receive the benefits of healing. Get to know the names of your clients, and some history about them. Also networking with other holistic professionals, community groups, professional organizations and such, improves your standing in the community and spreads the word about your valuable healing practice. Greeting your clients each time by shaking hands, when you see them personalizes them, and it gives you the opportunity to tune into their physical presence. As you physically connect with your clients you create a one-on-one bond that depends the client healer relationship.

Just as important as it is to greet your clients, it is equally important to make yourself available to answer their questions about the healing treatments, protocols, procedures, etc.

Two final techniques that can encourage client retention have to do with each individual's self-awareness as a healer.

First an honest assessment of how much time and energy you are wiling to spend on networking, teaching classes, workshops or lecturing, and cultivating a clientele.

Burnout and boredom are energy zappers that can sneak up on you and rob you of your passion for healing. By remaining present while doing healings you avoid the healing from becoming routine, you keep yourself fresh and alive.

If you find yourself not being present or going through the motions as a routine, it may be time for a little quiet reflection as to where your healing practice is going.

A second technique for fostering greater self-awareness is committing to your own personal education.

How often do you take seminars, classes or workshops?

Being inspired by another healer can help to further your own healing abilities. Taking a workshop, class or attending training can refresh your spirit as well as avail you of new healing techniques to apply in your own healing practice/business.

As you stay fresh your staff and clients.

As you try some of these techniques for yourself, you will see which ones work well for you and match with your personality, and personal goals as a holistic healer.

Trust your intuition as you connect with your clients on a deeper level and watch as they become more committed to their own healing journey. And in the process of healing your clients on this journey, watch your business/practice grow and prosper. perceive that energy and will recommit to their jobs and their healing journey.

Chapter 5

Marketing

There are countless simple, effective and low-cost ways for you to promote your holistic healing services without going broke in the process.

Here's ten fast and easy ways to get you started:

1. Always be prepared with an "elevator speech". When you meet new people talk about the benefits associated with receiving holistic healing - NOT the actual techniques you use to achieve the outcome. In a nutshell, let prospective clients know how you solve their problems, not how you do it.

2. Network often and set goals. When attending events, workshops or meetings, don't sit by people you know. The point is to meet new people! Make a goal of meeting 3-5 new people at each event. The key to effective networking is to build relationships and be interested in others; get their business cards and ask questions about their business.

3. Joining various clubs or groups is another way to promote your massage business. Every community has numerous organizations, such as a chamber of commerce, Rotary that is excellent places to meet people and talk about what you do. But don't join if you are not going to participate. Simply being on a group's mailing list will not help you build the kind of relationships that generate sales or promote interest in your business.

4. A great way to meet people is to volunteer in your community. Other volunteers will generally ask what you do. Wearing a shirt with your business name will be a reminder of the services you provide.

5. Teach a class through the local community education program. Community education programs attract people throughout your service area. Doing this will help you make contacts and also establish you as an expert in your field.

6. Ask for referrals! There is nothing wrong with asking your current clients if they know of others who might benefit from your healing therapy services. You might consider creating a "refer a friend" discount coupon for your clients to give to friends and family.

7. Create strategic alliances with other professionals with non-competing businesses. As a healing therapist you may want to develop a relationship with a chiropractor, a massage therapist, or an acupuncturist for example. Anyone who shares your target market would be a great candidate.

8. Write a press release announcing your new business, advanced certifications or to let the community know about an industry conference you've recently attended. Most newspapers have a business section and they are always looking for stories on local small businesses.

9. Take advantage of your e-mail. You never know where you emails are going to end up. Make sure to include a `signature line' in your e-mail that includes your business contact information including a website if you have one.

10. Establish a website presence. Today people surf the web for information on almost all the products and services they buy. For just a few dollars you can post a tremendous amount of information about your services, background and expertise on a basic website.

The bottom line is this; marketing your healing business will definitely require some time and creativity, but it doesn't mean you need to spend a ton of money. Put these marketing tips into action today and watch your appointment book soon fill up!

Here are 11 inexpensive ways to market your holistic practice:

1) Have a compelling response to the question "What do you do?" or "Tell me about yourself" Make it brief and interesting. If you only have 30 seconds, give them enough of an idea about what you do so that they seek you out to hear more later. Even in a situation where you have more time, be brief but to the point and then allow them to ask questions. Their questions will give you an idea of their particular interest.

2) Join or create a Holistic Chamber of Commerce. Find or create a group that has members with businesses aimed at a similar target market to yours.

Job seekers find others looking in the same industries.
(View: www.washingtonstateholisticchamberofcommerce.org)

3) Use every social occasion as a networking opportunity. Have your business cards ready if someone asks for one.

4) Offer to give a talk at a business meeting or teach a course at a school or training center. Use your expertise to generate interest in you and/or your holistic business.

5) Put an article about you or your business in a local newspaper. Local papers are often eager to print information about people in the area. Introduce yourself to the editor or person at your local paper who is responsible for press releases. Find out the information required for the article and learn to write a press release for newspapers.

6. **Form a networking partnership with others. If there are other businesses related to yours, seek them out and establish your own relationships. For example if you are a massage therapist you will want to form partnerships with medical doctors, chiropractors, physical therapists etc. Refer to your network partners and they in turn will refer to you.**

7. **Make a list of testimonials from customers to use with potential customers or use on your web site. Make these testimonials part of your brochure.**

8. **Model what you sell. If you are a web designer, have a spectacular website. If you sell clothes make sure your own fashion statement is flawless and creates the appropriate image.**

9. **Use a domain name that tells what your business is.**

10. **Create a unique style or logo that make you memorable. Establish yourself or your logo as a brand so people remember you.**

11. **Be grateful to those who refer business to you. Give them a gift or thank you card to show your appreciation.**

12 Marketing Tips for The Holistic Practitioners

Most holistic therapists ask me what is the best "advertising" to increase my business. To be honest no advertising formula exists that works for everyone
But what I can tell you is that marketing consists of three categories:
1. Ads you purchase
2. Free publicity you generate
3. Promotion in-house that you create yourself

Before you embark on any marketing adventure, review the following tips. These steps will save you money, time and effort:

1) Create a Marketing Plan:
Setting up a marketing plan, will have you identify your target market and figure out the best way to reach it. Remember to always keep your goals for your target market clear.

2) Clean up Your Practice:
Take a day, to clean and refresh your healing space, change the energy inside your space and do this every 3 months or so. If you have products you sell move them around. Walk outside and come into your office as through you were a new client coming for the first time. Pay attention to the sights, smells and sensations that you experience. Advertising is primary; it will bring clients to you, if you have something to tell people about. "Like

what new healing modality have you learned recently. "? What new healing tools do you have for sale, etc?

3) Train Your Staff:
A good staff keeps clients returning. And remember start with yourself.

Are you cheerful, happy and helpful?
Do you value your clients?
Your employees learn their attitudes from you.
Have you laid out standards for dress, behavior, punctuality and lunch breaks, etc.

Having a clearly laid out employee manual will create a clear understanding of what is expected on the job. Create a training approach that taken the individuality of the worker, and gives them the opportunity to learn at their own pace. Each staff member will learn differently, some need written notes, some need a verbal approach, and some require both approaches. Train you staff to treat your clients like the special people they are.

4) Create Events:
Doing educational seminars, classes and workshops in the community brings you practice attention and potential new clients.

5) Partner with local Charities:
You will get more media attention when you partner with a local non-profit organization on your events. I have offered free 15-minute readings or mini-healings sessions to people who join the local non-profit (MRS) Metaphysical Research Society or the Spokane chapter of the Washington State Holistic Chamber of Commerce. Thus the organizations gains members, and I gain potential clients and exposure to its membership. Pick a charity and make it your own. Join its board of directors and make a difference in your community. You and your practice will become better known, your public trust will rise, and you will help a local no-profit organization in the process.

6) Send Out Press Releases:
This is a great marketing tool, so get to know your local areas, newspapers, magazines, TV stations, radio stations disc jockeys. When possible get to know what specific reporters like to cover in the community, which ones are health conscious, open minded and interested in alternative medicine and Metaphysics. The send them tailored press releases.

7) Read the following books to gain insight into promoting, and marketing your business:
- The Anatomy of Buzz by Emanuel Rosen
- Guerilla Marketing by Jay Conrad
- The Seven Laws of Money by Michael Phillips
- The Secrets of Word of Mouth Marketing by George Silverman

- The Soul of Money by Lynne Twist

8) Know Your Neighbors:
Walk the neighborhood where you practice is located, and handout flyers, business cards, brochures, etc. Talk to those you meet. The direct contact gives those you meet a face to associate with your practice. Remember the personal approach is invaluable. If there is a local merchants association, join and advertise in their publication. (See AHANA.org)

9) Create incentives:
Offer clients a free session for every 3 clients they refer that pay you. Send out birthday cards to long time clients offering them a free session or discount off their next session. Offer a discount on products you sell to long-term clients.

10) Create a web site:
A web site is a calling card to the world, and a way for the local community to find you.

11) Forgive:
Forgive yourself for your mistakes, forgive your clients for being late occasionally, and forgive your staff for minor errors they commit. Forgiveness leads to trust and trust leads to honesty. Be honest with yourself and others and it will come back to you ten fold.

12) Joy:
Create fun at work, have a sense of humor. Being happy with your staff and clients keeps everyone in a good mood and elevates their vibration. Life is to short not to be happy.

Developing a Holistic Marketing Plan

Many holistic healing professionals begin a practice by marketing haphazardly never really knowing what they are going to do next or why. This is understandable since most service professionals do not have an understanding of marketing and how a marketing plan can help them. However, marketing a practice without a plan can be a huge detriment to your success in private practice.

The idea of developing a holistic marketing plan is often scary and overwhelming for most healing professionals. They often don't know where to start or what is involved in developing a plan and therefore avoid it and/or convince themselves that they don't need one.

The fact is, however, that most successful businesses do have a plan. After all, if you don't know where you are going, how will you know how to get there?

The good news is that most holistic healing professionals don't need a complicated marketing plan. Make it easy on yourself and develop a simple plan that you know you will utilize. There is no point in developing something that is not going to be used.

7 ELEMENTS OF A HOLISTIC MARKETING PLAN

1) Market Research

You will need to do some sort of analysis of your market. Who is providing services similar to you? Where are they located? What prices are they charging? Are there gaps in their services that you could perhaps fill?

Further, it's important that you assess the demand for your services. Are there people who want and need your services? Is there room in the market for another professional offering services like yours?

2) Select Your Target Audience(s)

focusing on a specific target market is an important part of being successful in your business. Most professionals resist narrowing in on a specific market often because they fear they will close the door on other potential clients. In reality, however, the more narrow your market, the easier it is to get known for what you do, and ultimately the more clients you will have.

Furthermore, many cities these days have an abundance of helping and healing professionals. If you are going to stand out from the crowd, you will have to market to a specific and unique population.

3) Identify Your Purpose and Goals

What are your goals for marketing your practice? You must be specific and quantify the results you want to achieve. For example, how many clients do you want to attract, and by when? How much income do you want to bring in? How many clients will you need to do this?

Your goals must be concrete, realistic and measurable. They should include those that are short-term (3-12 months) as well as those that are long term (1-5 years). A marketing plan is intended to be fluid, so don't worry about setting goals too far into the future. They can be modified as necessary.

4) Create Your Holistic Marketing Message

Once you have your target market identified you will need to write a marketing message--a statement of who you work with, what kinds of problem(s) you help solve, the benefits of your services, some proof (i.e. testimonials) that you can help clients solve their problem(s), and a call to action, inviting them to do something (e.g. to contact you for more information).

Many therapists and healing professionals are reluctant to be this specific about their services. However, unless you are very clear on your marketing message, you will likely find all aspects of marketing that follow this step challenging.

Clarity is key when it comes to marketing. It's important to be able to articulate your services both verbally and in writing if you want to communicate effectively with potential clients.

5) Choose Your Marketing Strategies & Develop a Time Line

Describe the marketing methods you will use to attract your clients. These can include networking, public speaking, writing articles, advertising, direct mail, or any method you use to let others know about your services.

Once you select your marketing strategies, the next step is to put them into a very specific plan of action. What exactly will you do and by when? For example, one marketing strategy might be that you will send out a brochure, letter and/or flyer to all the people in your network announcing your practice, or reminding them of it. You would specify a date when you would do this and then perhaps a date for following up with them via phone.

6) Establish Your Budget

Examine your finances carefully and conduct some research on what it will cost you for each marketing method that you choose. It is a good idea to keep your costs as low as possible by selecting marketing strategies that are free or low cost--especially when you are first starting your practice and funds may be low. Many of the best strategies for marketing a practice are free.

You will have to budget for marketing materials i.e. brochure, website, etc. and perhaps for mailing costs if you plan on doing any direct mail strategies. Other expenses you may incur include costs for advertising, letterhead, envelopes, office rental, and costs of running your office.

7) Track and Modify Your Results

Keep track of the results of your marketing efforts so that you can evaluate and modify your strategies accordingly. This way you will know exactly how effective they are at bringing in clients.

If after a while your marketing strategies are not creating the results you desired, you will have to modify the strategies, or choose alternative methods.

During my life's journeys I have met many gifted and wonderful holistic practitioners, but most of them had no idea how to market themselves or operate a successful business. Here are some suggestions to help you spend your dollars wisely, and market yourself with integrity.

Having a clear, concise message operates successful holistic businesses. Your business depends upon using the appropriate, consistent photos, fonts, and logo. Remember unprofessional brochures, business cards and web sites turn potential clients away. Hire a professional (Trade Services if possible) and get it right the first time, saving you money and time having to redo it. Consistency is the key. Hone your message, and business logo until it feels right intuitively, and then stick with it. Remember that it takes seven times for potential clients to see your message (Ad) before they call for an appointment. Patience and persistence pay in print advertising. Give weekly publications a month, monthly publications a year, quarterly publications, a year, and annual publications 3 years to perform. Market directly to your specific audience; take the time to explore options and avenues that specifically target your client base in your community. When you make a decision on advertising, set an intention as you write the check. Ask the Universe for a return on your investment.

Here are a few more holistic marketing tips:

Track your Advertising, ask each caller, each e-mailer these 3 questions:

1) How did you hear about me?

2) Where did you find my phone number?

3) Where did you find my web site? Referrals from other clients are also an effective form of advertising, so give incentives to your current clients to spread the word about your business i.e.; discount on their next session, a free session for every (3-5) clients that they refer to you that have paid for a session, a gift certificate the client can use for themselves or give away as a gift. Embrace the power of the written word. You are expert at what you do. Spread your knowledge.

Articles in print and web publications give you credibility while generating new clientele. Lectures, Workshops and speaking engagements create a "buzz" about your work. When necessary get professional help in getting your message out to the public, your image is important to conveying your work and knowledge. Try to have your business card, brochures, flyers, stationary and other business materials all with your logo, web site address and phone number.

Remember abundance is infinite, go forward and enjoy the
fruits of your work, you deserve it.

Intuitive Marketing for The Holistic Entrepreneur

Intuitive Marketing is a term for hands on, low cost approach to marketing/promoting the holistic business owner.

Building a holistic healing business/practice whether it is a massage, reiki, spiritual healing, quantum touch, chiropractic, or medical intuition, is along term endeavor. Even with the growing popularity of holistic healing or alternative healing, you can't just hang out a sign and have clients lining up to see you.

Intuitive Marketing is about using your "gut feelings" or intuitive nature to let your community know about your healing services, your healing business.

This requires organizing yourself, making a plan of action, using your intuition to sense the directions to go, and committing to carrying out the plan of action.

Then taking this plan out to your community, by shaking hands, putting up flyers, networking, handing out business cards, talking with people doing classes, workshops, lectures and letting everyone see the passion and enthusiasm in your eyes, and feel the passion and enthusiasm for your healing services.

Have enthusiasm with person you talk to about your healing services.
If you allow that enthusiasm to wane, or be less than when you first begun doing this valuable work, what impression will that diminished enthusiasm have on those you talk to? Will they want to use your services?

Whenever you do intuitive marketing, don't forget your enthusiasm and passion. Let it shine out from your eyes and your very being. This is important as we discuss "Intuitive Marketing Strategies" because these strategies will NOT WORK without passion and enthusiasm.

Also don't think you can do Intuitive Marketing for a few weeks or a month that is simply not enough. Any successful holistic business owner will tell you- even when you become successful you can't stop marketing your services.

My clients tell me they don't like selling themselves, neither do I. Marketing your holistic healing services is about bringing your healing abilities to the community, not selling your services.

The moment you find yourself selling your services, to convince someone they need them, you have lost contact with your passion. Stop! Offering your services is about attracting the clients that want to get well, that want to get well, that what wholeness in their life.

So lets review some popular Intuitive Marketing techniques:

1. Always put your picture on your business card, people relate to the visual of seeing someone's picture on a business card. Especially a healer.
2. Stamp on the back of your business card a coupon with 10% off the first visit.
3. Have your vehicle window painted with your business address, logo, phone number and web site address
4. In addition to your web site, make sure you have an answering machine or voice message system that offers information such as; hours of operation, directions to your office, types of services offered, and fees.

Ask your clients for referrals, and offer them an incentive for referring new clients to you.

5. Joining the local holistic or regular chamber of commerce, or local holistic healers network. Remember Network, Network, and Network.
6. Do free lectures on your healing modalities.
7. Offer workshop and classes on your healing modalities, teach people self-care, and educate them.
8. Create an email newsletter.
9. Position yourself as an expert on Reiki, Spiritual Healing, or whatever healing methods you use in your business.
10. Do expos, health fairs, farmers markets, etc. Submit articles to your local papers, magazine extolling the benefits of alternative healing.

The bottom line is people can't use your services if they don't know you offer them. So go out there and tell the world about your healing services.

In order to understand intuitive selling, it is necessary to understand the concept of the unconscious and the ego. These two parts of human consciousness determine much of our behavior, thoughts and attitudes. They are also important in understanding how we relate to others. They determine how we act on the surface and on a deeper level we cannot recognize consciously. Without getting too analytical, following is a brief description of the ego (conscious self) and the unconscious (inner self) and how they relate to your sales activities. Take time to explore this area further. It will bring tremendous value to your sales career. Go Inside to the Unconscious The first step to understand the outside world better and to know what success means to you is to get in touch with your inner self or the unconscious. The unconscious is the part of human beings that is intuitive. It is the power behind all human intentions and actions, providing us with dreams, creativity and imagination. It is who you really are at the core of your being and gives you purpose.
Why do dreams seem so real? The mind does not know the difference. This is an expression of the power of the unconscious. Your greatest challenge to becoming more intuitive in your selling and more successful in your career is to get in touch with the unconscious and listen to its direction. This will help you stay on target

toward living your mission and goals and making the proper decisions as you respond to customers and the environment around you. The goals and mission are your internal compass, or steering wheel, in making daily and weekly decisions about your sales activities. As you make these decisions, step back, listen to your inner voice and keep them connected with your mission statement and goals. Trust the message of the unconscious; this is intuitive selling. People may enjoy their work -- some people are actually having more fun at work than play. However, most people would rather be doing something else. This is true because many people are not doing the work they love -- or work they were meant to do (what their unconscious wants them to do).

The unconscious needs a mission or goal. It can't wander, unless that is your goal or mission. Your greatest job in life is to find that mission and remove unwanted thoughts or things that are not true to that mission. The Ego We has a lot to learn from children. Young children have a high degree of contentment about them and the ability to bounce back from disappointment with ease, which comes from lack of ego. Also, anyone who has ever competed in sports knows that in order to function at the highest level of ability, he/she must get into the zone. Athletes must remove their egos and operate on instinct or intuition. They must operate from their unconscious. The ego is the conscious mind. It is the voice in our heads that is critical or "parent-like." The ego is focused on rewarding itself and not helping others. It acts as a barrier to the pure messages that come from the unconscious. Thus, the terms "ego-maniac" or "big ego" are used to describe people who function solely from their egos.

This type of functioning leads to imbalance and selfishness, two of the biggest barriers to selling success. You cannot possibly find ways to help customers and be a great listener if you are functioning from the ego. Self-discipline can contain the ego and quiet its voice. The concepts you will read about in this book, if put into practice, can help you move away from ego-centric behaviors, which ultimately leads to better intuitive skills and a closer connection to the core of who you are, which is in the unconscious. The ego has a need to control and the false perception that things can be made safe through control. Let go of your need for control; it's too stressful and many times can lead to the opposite of the intended result. This leads to difficulties with change.

The ego tends to fight change through fear and worry. The best way to deal with change is to realize that your unconscious is immutable. It is who you are. Eliminate Negative Self-Talk The ego is the creator of negative self-talk and fear. The unconscious listens to your self-talk and takes action on what it hears or sees. This is why it is so important to avoid negative people and events. Identify negative influences and remove yourself from them. Negative thoughts, images, and people hold you back from achieving your potential by influencing and programming your powerful unconscious. The unconscious needs only positive influences. Find Quiet Time Communicating with the powerful inner parts of your consciousness is difficult, but not impossible.

The unconscious needs quiet time to work and express itself. Meditation, prayer or just sitting alone is excellent ways to quiet your mind and let thoughts emerge from your unconscious. This is not a quick-fix process and it takes time to develop the proper skills. There are many programs that can assist you in these areas and if used wisely and with discretion, can have positive results. Perceptions are Reality We see the world in two ways: the way we think things are and through the value we assign to those things. Work on changing your perception of how things are to produce big changes in your life. You create your own reality. Your unconscious is the key player in this. This is also true of your customers, who develop perceptions of you and your value to them and their organization. Being in tune with your unconscious is an excellent way of keeping your perceptions more clear and obtaining a better understanding of the perceptions others have of you. Self-Image how you see yourself equals the results you get in return. What is your self-image? Where is your internal barometer set?

Intuitive Selling for The Holistic Entrepreneur

Picture yourself the way you want to be and set specific goals to improve your self-image.

Determine and write down your specific goals and personal mission statement to be sent to your unconscious.

These goals must be written down; if not, they will randomly move through your ego and conscious mind, rather then programming your unconscious mind.

Be around successful people, copy them and add your own personal touch, which improves what they do.

Follow the advice of winners and do not just listen and do nothing. They are winners for a reason.

Let go of your ego and take action on self-improvement based on what you have learned from winners

There is plenty of room at the top and success is lasting, otherwise it is not success. How would you act if there were no chance of failure? Act this way.
Visualize your success and focus on the end results, or actions, you will be doing when success comes. · Remove limiting thoughts about success.

Do not say, "I need to be"; rather, say, "I am this person."

Visualize how you expect to be in the future and begin acting that way today. If sales is your profession, then realize that selling is extremely valuable and a service that helps people. It is fun, rewarding, and fulfilling to help others.

Action Steps:

- Learn more about the ego and the unconscious.

- Make time for quiet moments, with no interruptions, and let your mind be silent.

- Listen to the messages about your life's purpose from your inner self.

- Ask how you can create a personal mission that serves others

- Begin living this mission.

- Learn to control the ego and to release your true inner self. This is the key to happiness and to developing intuitive selling abilities.

Marketing Healing Vibrations

Recently while retuning the organs of a client (with tuning forks) the idea came to me that my business is like a tuning fork in that it sends out vibrations in the form of marketing energy.

My marketing efforts are vibrational patterns, sounds emanating out into the community, the world.

I have spent 25 years building a successful channeling, healing and educational centre (the Family of Light Centre) based upon creating healing opportunities for clients seeking health and wholeness.

The strategic marketing efforts I have used have created the success I now enjoy.

So now let me share with you these vibrational marketing practices.

1) Strategic Marketing:
Strategic marketing is using your intuition, your intuitive nature (gut feeling) to understand your clients needs, desires and designing your healing business to meet their needs.

2) Know Your Healing Journey:
You must have a clear mission of your healing business. Use your business identity as a decision making tool to help you advance your mission. Know your healing journey by clarifying your mission and living it.

<u>3) Define your goals:</u>
<u>Setting goals and make them measurable, so you can see results will help you maximize your marketing impact. Your measure of success should integrate values and purpose for offering healing services.</u>

<u>4) Know Your Target Audience:</u>
Always place your clients needs at the top of your business goals. Listening to client's needs and desires will enhance your understanding of the treatment plans necessary for the client's to achieve wellness.

Remember marketing your holistic healing business is about creating a relationship with each client, and building a lifelong relationship of mutual respect, caring and understanding. Doing so insures your business success for years.

<u>Marketing For Success</u>

Here are a few things you and your staff should be doing to help support your business.

Business Identity: Logo, slogan, graphic ok? Consistency is the important issue. Do people identify with your logo, slogan, or the graphics you use in print ads, brochures, posters, etc.

Business Cards: They should have the contact information necessary for clients to reach you and understand what you do. i.e. Phone numbers, email, website, address and what you offer, services, products.

Signs: Inside and outside your business, sidewalk signs, welcoming entrance sign, thanks for visiting us on exit. Come up with creative signs, which express your services or products.

Press Kits: A press kit does not have to be fancy, but it must have your name, contact information, you (or your stores) history/background, a photo of you or your business, frequency asked questions about your business.

Photographs: Make it a professional looking picture.

Brochures: A simple black and white beauty, that lists all the products or services you offer, with a picture of you, your staff and office included if possible.

Events Calendar: You want these sent on a regular basis to all your clients, posted in your business, and places around town and on your website.

Website: A must, should be clearly designed, fast download, easy to use, and your business information.

Misconceptions in Marketing

Holistic healing professionals often have many misunderstandings about what marketing is and how it works. This can be a major problem as any misconceptions you hold about marketing can seriously impair your ability to attract clients effectively. They can interfere with your ability to focus, consume your energy, cause procrastination, and erode your self-confidence.

The good news is that it doesn't have to be this way. Once misconceptions are identified and replaced with accurate information, you can become more energized, focused, and optimistic about your ability to build a practice. Furthermore, once these shifts take place, you start getting much better results from your marketing efforts.

Misconception #1:
You can build a practice without learning marketing strategies and skills.

While some professionals succeed at building a practice without a lot of experience or training in marketing, often their success is due to having a large network of people who know and trust them, or a few good referral sources that consistently send them clients.

Marketing, after all, is largely about building lasting relationships with many people over time. To do this, you have to know how to go about finding the people you will market to, and know the best ways to deliver your message to them so that you are perceived as having a service that is valuable to them. You will also need to know effective methods for staying in touch with these people so that you can build strong relationships with them.

Misconception #2:
If you are a skilled holistic health practitioner, you will automatically be successful at building a practice.

It certainly will help you in building a practice if you are skilled at what you do, as some of your clients that have benefited from your services will tell others about their experiences with you.

However, it is possible to be excellent at what you do and never achieve the kind of success that you want. Your success at filling your practice will depend on many factors that go well beyond your skills as a practitioner.
Some of these factors include how strong your desire is to succeed, the extent of your visibility, how effective you are at choosing and implementing marketing strategies, your persistence and patience, and how quickly you learn from your mistakes.

Misconception #3:
It is only necessary to market your services when you begin your practice.

When you first start to build a practice you will likely need to spend a great deal of time marketing. The amount of time will depend on your goals (e.g. how many clients you want and how quickly you want to build your practice).

As your client load increases, you can gradually cut back somewhat on the amount of time you spend marketing. The mistake that many people make, however, is to quit marketing all together once they start having enough - or close to enough - clients. The problem with this is that clients continuously come and go, often without much warning.

If you set aside time for marketing on a regular basis, you will avoid the feast and famine cycle that many professionals get caught in.

Misconception #4:
Promotional materials should begin by focusing on you and your credentials.

Too often helping professionals develop marketing materials (e.g. brochures, flyers, and websites) that immediately focus on who they are and their credentials. While potential clients do want to know about you, they are usually more interested at first to learn if you understand the problems they are experiencing and whether you can help them solve them.

If your marketing materials begin by identifying specific problems and the benefits you clients can expect, you will be more likely to attract their attention so that they continue reading, and perhaps even pick up the phone and call you for more information. You will need good, strong text that is written from a marketing perspective to entice your clients to take action on your offer.

Misconception #5:
If a marketing strategy gets minimal response, it's best to try something else.

Many healing professionals assume that all they have to do when starting a practice is run an ad or send out some letters once to a few referral sources and clients will come pouring in. When this doesn't happen, they become discouraged and may assume that that strategy is not an effective one.

It is true that some marketing methods may not be the best ones for you and your particular situation. However, there are many things that influence whether a particular strategy will be effective for you and your target market. If you find that you are not getting the results you intended, it may be because you giving up too soon.

Most strategies have to be implemented repeatedly and be fine-tuned as you learn what works and what doesn't. Successful marketing requires testing and tweaking the methods you use until you get the results you want. If you have given a particular method a fair trial and it still isn't working for you, then it's probably a good idea to try something else.

Misconception #6:
You can be all things to all people.

Believing that by marketing to everyone you will increase your chances of getting clients is another common misconception of healing professionals. This belief often stems from a fear that you won't attract enough clients if you don't market to everyone. One of the major problems with trying to market to everyone is that you end up blending in with all the other professionals in your field.

By choosing a distinct target market and a specific niche as your focus, you will be able to stand out from the crowd. Potential clients will have an easier time finding you and it will be easier for you to know where to find them as well. In addition, it is a lot easier to become known for what you do when you focus in this way.

Misconception #7:
You can build a successful practice without planning.

Professionals sometimes attempt to build a practice by dabbling haphazardly with a few marketing methods now and again. The problem with this is that it's difficult to get somewhere if you don't know where you are going.

When you don't plan and structure when and how you will market, you won't know how much time you will need to spend marketing, you will have difficulty building and maintaining momentum, and it will be difficult for you to track your results.

Careful planning can counter a lot of the frustration, fear and doubts you may have about being successful. The more clear and specific your plan is, the better you will be able to implement it as you will always know what your next step is.

The more accurate information you have about marketing, the fewer of the above misconceptions you will have. This in turn will lead to much faster and better results, not to mention a much more enjoyable experience building your healing business.

Misconception #8:
Forgiveness of Oneself and Clients

One must learn to cultivate the forgiveness of not only one's self, but of your client's. For in using forgiveness in your business relations with your clients and yourself you will build, an understanding of the human factor of making mistakes on the path of one's life.

Promoting Your Self with Integrity

Do you need a new way to promote yourself?

How about a way to promote yourself focusing on relationship building?

Many of us, who feel passionate about our holistic business, are overwhelmed when it comes to promotion, advertising and marketing ourselves. We believe we have to sell our services and push our products onto people who don't want them, but this is rarely the case. In fact it is difficult to sell something to someone else when they don't want it. The image of a typical salesperson is loud, obnoxious, and unconscious of them and others. They manipulate to get what they want and sell us something we don't need.

Who wants to be a part of all that?

No wonder we feel insecure and unsure when we present ourselves to the public.

We wish our clients would miraculously magnetize themselves to us and we'd wait by the phone and take appointments. Unfortunately, that rarely works. Yes, we need to put ourselves and our services out there - but the good news is we can magnetize others who value our services.

The key to this is to understand that marketing is nothing more than building relationships. When you build on a relationship and the customer trusts you, and is in control, they won't feel manipulated or pushed into a sale. We all know buying decisions come from an emotional buying decision. That we must take care of all the objections and answer them so that we can get our prospect excited about our holistic services. So if we know that buying is emotional, why don't we sell with our own emotions? We must use our heart, as well as our mind when related to our clients.

We want our customers to connect emotionally with us, yet we don't expect to become emotionally involved with them.

Why not?

Wouldn't you trust your friend more than a stranger with your money?

When we try to find something in common, or just listen to them and genuinely care about them, then they will sense our support and open up with questions, and be emotionally ready to you your services, resulting in more clients.

But it must be authentic. Nothing will make our clients will feel manipulated and force them to run in the other direction than a false sense of interest from us.

See yourself in service, be authentic, be your best caring self. Mean it. And most of all, take your time. This is promoting with integrity.

If you want to be successful in promoting your business, there is really only one rule to follow. Focus on your customer instead of on yourself. It sounds simple, but most of us focus on what services we have to offer, and our business, instead of our clients' needs.

Public Presentations For the Holistic Practitioner

When I became a sound healer, I was already an accomplished channeler and holistic therapist. I realized that Sound Healers could offer more than just a healing treatment to their clients. As a group I believe that sound healers like most holistic healers are passionate about helping people and improving their quality of health and well-being.

As a presenter or public speaker on holistic healthcare you can touch the lives of thousands of people in only one or two hours.

Public presentations offer numerous personal and professional benefits for your holistic practice. For one a speaker typically receives some monetary compensation per presentation. If additional income appeals to you, doing public presentations might be just right for you.

I co-direct the Family of Light Healing Centre, but also promote myself as a public speaker on Metis Shamanism, Sound healing and Holistic Healthcare. Besides the potential for extra income from public presentations there are other professional benefits. Doing public presentations provides name recognition. It sets you above the competition. Even if the presentation is free, when an organization hires you to preset, it conveys a sense of endorsement. As a speaker on holistic healthcare you must be an expert and a very great practitioner.

Doing public presentations puts you in front of potential clients, and because they have come to hear your presentation to learn, their natural sales resistance is lowered.

For example my presentation may focus on "Medical Intuition" Self Care. Self-care employs any combination of techniques that I teach in my workshop or explain in my book "Medical Intuition Handbook", such as self-scanning or scanning with a partner, or using a pendulum to read the chakras.

Or I may do a demonstration using specific frequency tuning forks for specific ailments, i.e.; tenses muscles, cramped muscles, knots.

Since nothing can replace a professional healing session with you, the audience will automatically think of you when seeking holistic healthcare.

Remember the marketing opportunities extend beyond the presentation itself.

Here are 3 ways:

1. Most organizations hosting your presentation will publicize the event.

2. Promote yourself as a holistic health care teacher. It is a natural extension of public presentations. There are certain techniques that I do not teach in my presentations because they are difficult to do in a large setting. However, I easily teach these techniques in my workshops and classes.

3. Doing Public Presentation allows you to market other products or services.

For example I am able to promote the Family of Light Healing Centre
And the products and services the Centre offers.

If you are not affiliated with holistic healthcare facility, find one that would be willing to pay for referrals or pay you a nominal fee for mentioning their facility or handing out their promotion material at your presentations.

Continual exposure is everything. Potential clients are everywhere, so go out and do as many presentations as possible in your community.

Public Presentations:
How to Market Your Professionalism

I am going to focus on the steps necessary to promote your self and your public presentations:

1. Take inventory of your unique healing skills, knowledge and educational background.
2. Research what work environments, career fields or organizations would seek your services.

3. **Why would they come to your presentations?**

    A. <u>Relief of symptom for specific condition</u>
    B. <u>Stress</u>
    C. <u>Injuries</u>
    D. <u>Health Maintenance</u>
    E. **Educational Expansion**

Now that you have taken inventory, design a program for your presentations. The key to a successful presentation is to keep the topic focused. Many simple holistic healthcare techniques such as yoga stretching, self-massage, using the nerve fork on tight muscles can be taught during presentations.

This list below is not all-inclusive, but it is a starting point.

- Meditation to relax, relive stress
- Basic yoga stretches to relieve tensions in the neck and shoulders
- Using the Nerve Tuning fork on overworked and tight muscles
- Sound healing how and why it works: An Overview
- Why healthcare maintained is important

Public Presentations: Where to Market Your Services

Now that we have discussed and laid out a proposed presentation plan, where do you market your public presentations:

- Health-food stores
- Wellness and fitness centers
- Health-care organizations
- Non-profit organizations
- Speakers Bureaus
- Trade shows/expos
- Professional associations
- Advocacy groups
- Local chamber of commerce
- Business associations & civic groups
- University extensions
- Church groups

And remember when doing your presentations to highlight key points with a question to your audience, such as, "What causes muscle cramps"? What percentage of people in America has chronic back-pain? Obviously you already know the answers, but the questions keep the audience involved and thinking about the subject matter.

Question and answer sessions are essential to any presentation, so be sure to allow adequate time.

Finally, compile key presentation points and use as a handout.

Besides offering a good presentation, you need to be a good speaker and an appreciative guest. Remember to thank the organization or host who invited you. Everyone likes to be thanked, especially in public.

Charging a fee for Presentations?

Should you charge a fee for your presentations? This is a question only you can answer.
But here are a few rules of thumb when calculating a possible fee.

- What would you make on an hourly basis doing your healing work?
- Preparation Time (two hours for every hour presentation)
- Travel time to and from the event
- Marketing costs (brochures, flyers, handouts)

Now that you have calculated all the considerations you have a fee base to work from.
Learn to negotiate and don't be afraid to walk away. And if you really want to speak before a group, but they can not afford to pay you your usual fee, consider a trade for services, such as:

- Videotape or audiotape your presentation. You can sell the tapes later.
- Print extra handouts or marketing material
- Provide a table/space & volunteer to sell your products before and after the event.
- Set up a special book signing event
- Free ads in their Newsletter or publication

I hope this series of article has inspired you to consider doing public presentations in your community.

Besides the professional benefits from doing a presentation there is no substitute for the natural high that comes from speaking in front of an audience, plus the applause and appreciation do wonders for your self-confidence.

8 Public Presentation Marketing Tips

1. Have a brochure on your public presentations
2. Create a short description of your presentations (use a catchy title)

3. <u>Always solicit testimonials and letters of recommendation. This will greatly enhance your future marketing material.</u>

4. <u>Put your face on your business card. It puts a face to a name. Remember you are selling yourself.</u>

5. <u>Dress for success. Casual but stylish</u>

6. <u>Network with other local presenters, form a mini speaker's bureau and pool your marketing resources.</u>

7. <u>Send press release to local newspapers, trade journals, etc.</u>

8. Don't forget to send a thank you to the organization or host who invites you.

Chapter 6

Advertising

Targeting Holistic Advertising Messages

To craft on-target messages, you have to know to whom you're writing. And the only way to do that is to know your client market. Follow the tips outlined below:

Tip 1. Attend holistic association meetings.
   One way to learn about holistic healthcare trends is to attend Expo's, professional organization meetings, seminars, and conferences. You'll pick up a great deal of information - including what your clients are saying about what they want from a holistic healthcare practitioner. I am a member of the Holistic Chamber of Commerce.

Tip 2. Become good friends with editors of trade publications.
   Trade publications are a great way to get information about the very people to whom you are marketing. Many publications conduct readership surveys. And, don't be afraid to call your advertising sales rep or editor and ask him or her for marketing tips and strategies.

Tip 3. Surf the Internet for relevant information.
   You can find a wealth of information about your clients and their pain points simply by researching the Internet. Don't understand insider jargon? Type "define: [word]" into Goggle for sites listing the definition.

Tip 4. Monitor discussion forums.

Want to know what your clients are saying the holistic healthcare field. Make it a point to visit holistic healthcare forums.

Visit sites like Holistic Junction.com, Self-Growth.com,   Healingwell.com, medical-intuitives.com, soulhealer.com,

Giving clients what they want is easy once you know to whom you're marketing. Do due diligence on your target audience, understand their pain points, and know which marketing tactics work best.

Your copy will be much more "on target."

And you will reach the audience you want those interested in the health of their self and family in a holistic manner.

Online Advertising?

Seven years ago few business people would have considered advertising on the World Wide Web.

Now if you are not advertising on the web you are missing a valuable opportunity to be found by computer savvy customers.

Using online Yellow Pages & Directories to search for products and services locally or nationwide has become more popular. Online yellow pages or Internet yellow pages are consumer friendly innovations that provide excellent local or nationwide search results with very little effort.

An example Yahoo! Get Local, with listings in more than 2,000 categories is the most popular online directory. It garned over 19 million visitors monthly in the second quarter of 2004, according to Nielsen/Net ratings.

Compared to laboriously thumbing thru hefty print yellow pages, the online search is quick and easy. Using the Internet to find a product or services is a fast growing trend. A 2003 study of online shopping in the USA, conducted by the Pew Internet & American Life Project, shows that nearly 2/3rds of Internet users are now online shoppers.

And a survey of Internet users released earlier this year by the Kelsey Group, a research firm, and Biz-Rate.com, an online shopping search engine notes that 44% of respondents performed more local searches online this year than in 2003.

So is the Internet advertising for you?

Only you can be the judge of that, but remember to get noticed you must stay ahead of the competition. Checking into the local Internet yellow pages or directory is a start. Many directories offer listings for free or a small fee. I personally have listings in dozens of directories.

Spreading the word about your business (products or services) is a must in this Global Village economy. If you do decide to do an online listing, have it listed with a link to your web site so you can track the results of where your ad was seen.

Remember at a time when e-shopping is growing by leaps and bounds, if you're not out there and easily findable in cyberspace you risk missing the opportunity to grow and prosper.

Advertising- VS- Publicity

Question:
What is the difference between publicity and advertising?

Answer:
Publicity is free and advertising is paid placement.

If you operate a business you will need both, however by using publicity you increase your exposure without increasing your advertising budget.

So how to create Publicity?

By educating the media about your holistic business on a consistent basis. When done effectively, this increases your credibility and visibility, which in turn attracts new clients.

To create an effective publicity campaign, you need to know what is newsworthy about your business, then take that information and transform it into a press release, article or other newsworthy document.

Then deliver it (e-mail, mail or in person) to the appropriate media contacts before their publication deadlines.

By becoming an expert in your filed of work the media will give free exposure in local publications, and when they are writing stories, on weight loss, meditation, how to relax, pain management, etc., they will contact you rather than your competition.

So what is newsworthy you ask?

Below I list 12 newsworthy angles that your business can use to create publicity:

- Launching new products or services
- Expanding your existing business
- Offering solutions to current "Hot Topics" in the media
- Grand Openings
- Celebrating your business anniversary
- Community Outreach projects
- Public speaking about your business (services or products)
- Serving on the board of a holistic chamber of commerce or non-profit

- Receiving an award
- Giving awards to others
- Charity or fundraising events your business sponsors
- **Sponsoring a workshop or class**

So as you can see there are ways to generate publicity for your holistic business. These ways are very cost effective, as they will cost little or nothing, just your time and imagination.

Chapter 7

Articles and Ideas

5 Habits For Enlightened Entrepreneurs

I believe the rise of alternative or complementary healthcare is a continual growth industry.
I see it exploding everywhere as indicated by things like corporate fitness programs that aim to reduce company healthcare costs, the growing popularity of eco-tourism in the retreat world, the increase of yoga studios worldwide, the lifestyle trend of colorful and comfortable yoga wear being worn on and off the mat.

So, if you are a holistic healer, or healthcare entrepreneur, how do you financially position your business to be a player in this multi-billion dollar industry? There are 5 financial habits practiced by successful holistic healthcare practitioners/entrepreneurs that can help anyone achieve success in the alternative healthcare marketplace.

Adopting these successful habits will require you to step out of your current financial comfort zone, and create a new set of results for your business.

Habit 1: *Create/Write Down Your Plan*

Write down a concrete vision of your business and financial goals in the form of a 1 year, 3 year and 10 year timeline.

Why you ask? The more you clarify your ideal future vision, the greater clarity you will have about how to grow your business.

When you clarify what it is you want, you invoke the powerful process of manifestation, whereby you attract people, situations and opportunities that will help you realize your future.

If you don't take the time to start with this first habit, you lose the opportunity to achieve success at it highest level possible.

If you want to operate a successful business you must understand that the business can only grow as successful as you are.

The more knowledge and exposure to educational opportunities create the financial success you seek.

Enlightened Entrepreneurs realize that the present is created from the future against a backdrop of the past. This means honoring the past, but the present is created from how much energy you focus on writing out possible and probable outcomes for your business to unfold in your future.

The more you dream life into your business and financial future, the more you will be giving the Universe clarity on what you really want.

Your daily routine of managing your business will be an affirmation of your future vision of success.

Habit 2: *Cash Flow Mastership*

Once you have written your financial and business goals, you take inventory of your current business statistics:

- Monthly cash flow
- Areas of greatest profit
- Review your bottom line

Your successful business growth depends on you continually reviewing your "bottom line" and masterminding new ways to improve your cash flow.

Remember 80% of businesses fail in the first 5 years and 96% in the first 10 years. The main reason for this is the lack of focus on short term-cash flow.

Successful small business entrepreneurs focus on their short-term cash flows.

If you can master creating new cash flows, you will have additional income to expand the business. Also once you have mastered one cash flow, the next one you focus on will be easier.

Habit 3: *Know Your Clients*

**Do you know what services or products your clients like and dislike?
The better you know and understand your clientele's wants, needs, desires, like and dislikes about your business services and products, the easier it is to create the growth you want your business to achieve.**

Habit 4: *Create Passive Income*

Successful entrepreneurs realize one must create as much residual income as possible. This can come from real estate, publishing books, CD's, DVD's, Reiki Attunements, licensing rights to Crystaline reiki, Vibrational Yoga, and creating an educational program.

The business owners that our happiest with their results are those that continually review themselves, their business, their goals, and the community they serve.

Habit 5: *Educational Growth*

A commitment to learning will be one of the quickest ways to achieve the results you want for you and your business.

When you make conscious decisions about your business on a financial level, you will see opportunities to expand your education and grow more effectively towards successful creation of your business.

Financially successful holistic practitioners focus on achieving their business financial goals, master short-term cash flow, continually educate themselves on the healthcare marketplace, and creating passive income.

The more knowledgeable you are about the marketplace you serve, the greater possibility of success for you and your business.

7 Powerful Principles For Business Success

Most holistic practices or businesses are small, but that does not mean the owners are small. One can have a holistic healing practice and be big. Size is not in the eye of the beholder, but in the conscious expression of the leader. As the owner of a healing practice, a small one, you can be big in intentions, big in desires, plans and passion. Your practice is determined by your attitude, not your finances. You are a source healing service for inner guidance. You are big to clients seeking healing and understanding of their illness. You are big to your employees. You are big in the community as a light of hope in the healing of illness, thru alternative methods.

As a leader you can be small in the size of your practice but still lead big. You are as big and successful as you believe. Your beliefs become reality simply by their sheer innate power. Beliefs are deeply held thoughts. Quantum physics tells us thoughts are energy. So with thoughts being energy, our energy or thought must be positive in order to attract success.

The bible says " Be it done unto you as you believe" (Matthew 9:29). Scientists have recently begun to prove what shamans have taught for centuries. The power of positive thoughts is the secret to success. Leaders who understand the power of thought are successful. They know the most important work they do takes place in the mind. These leaders know that keeping their thoughts positively focused is the key to their success. So you ask, how do you maintain this success, in the mist of lack, smallness and negative energy that surrounds most small businesses?

Below are 7 principles to assist you in creating and maintaining your bigness in operating a holistic healing practice, your life and being a leader in the community:

1. **Vision:** Your vision is an inner image of what you want your business or life to achieve.

2. **Intuition:** Use your intuition as a way to gaining insight into your life's challenges or business decisions.

3. **Communication: Communications is a key to operating a successful business and having lasting personal relationships. Speak from the heart with the intuitive guidance you receive to employees and friends. You can inspire others when you speak to their desires, to their heart.**

4. **Prosperity Consciousness:** Prosperity consciousness is thinking, speaking and acting from a knowing that you are already a leader, a visionary and successful business owner.

5. **Joy:** Being in joy filled is the way to all your desires. When you are feeling joy, you radiate it and others feel it. And respond to it. Joyful leaders radiate joy to inspire, uplift and create their employees, family and friends to find their joy.

6. **Connection with time:** Remember even the most powerful leaders take time, to refuel, refresh and rejuvenate them. Make taking time a priority. You must make time with yourself for meditating, doing vibrational yoga or just being quiet. You cannot impart wisdom, joy and inspiration to other people if you are feeling run down, worn out and depleted of energy.

7. **Gratitude: Showing gratitude for your success goes along way to setting an example for others to remember to appreciate the joy of being successful in life and business.**

Follow these 7 principles and you will succeed at all you do in life, at work and in the community.

9 Successful Ideas For the Holistic Entrepreneur

1) Go beyond service: Offer classes, workshops, products, and events to inform your clients of how to maintain their wellness.

2) Create a Community: Creating a community is important if you want your practice to grow and succeed. Let your office serve as a hub for the holistic wellness community.

3) Be Consistent: Consistency is one of the keys to success. Let your clients know your schedule, set events on a regular basis.

4) Create a Serene Environment: By creating a beautiful, sensual, serene environment you will bring your clients back for more.

5) Take a Holiday: As much as you love your practice, remember to relax, rest, and rejuvenate yourself on a regular basis.

6) Re-evaluate: Regularly re-evaluate your services, products, classes and events.

7) Develop a web site: You must have a web site, it is your calling card to the holistic wellness community. A web site opens up a new world of potential clients looking for your services.

8)Don't become Complacent: Stay informed, read trade magazines, attend seminars, workshops, check out other practitioners offices, look at websites, listen to your clients, and host an open house event once a year.

9) Show appreciation: Express gratitude for your success. Give back to the community you serve.

Use these 9 Successful ideas and watch your business grow and prosper.

7 Rules for Attracting Abundance

1. Power
I am an extremely powerful person, here to impact people's lives profoundly. I am terrific at what I do.
Now, this isn't about my ego. My statement speaks to opening yourself up and receiving the truth of who you really are, owning your greatness, and putting yourself out there in a big way. Shamelessly. With pride.
You are an extremely powerful person.
And if you're not showing up to life in a way that reflects your true greatness, you need to ask yourself why not.
Life *begs* you to.
You will not attract everything you really want until you respect and express your greatness -- the truth of who you really are -- and become irresistibly attractive to yourself.

2. Truth

Living a meaningful life is about living a happy life. Living a happy life is about living your personal truth. The more you live your life in accord with what's true for you, the happier you will be and the better the things that you will attract.
Where are you not living what's true for you? Say it out loud to yourself. Yes, say it.
Note: Don't confuse your beliefs with truth. Beliefs are learned, truth just *is*.

3. The truth will set you free.
It takes tremendous courage to put aside our beliefs and to live the truth. The truth requires faith. The truth requires change. And sometimes, the truth just plain sucks. But the freedom truth allows is well worth the price.
Truth is a prerequisite for attraction.

4. Solitude.

To find the truth, we need time. Alone Time. Most of us don't experience anywhere near enough time for ourselves, the still point in a moving world where we can see our true reflection. And that needs to change if we are to use the incredible power of attraction.

5. Wasting Time

Okay, so time doesn't really exist -- it's made up. What we really need is more space. We are surrounded by too much clutter, stimulation, and noise. Who we are and what's important to us gets lost in all the racket.

When we have no space in our lives, our heads are down while we bull forward to get everything done, stiff-arming all the messages the Universe continually sends us -- what we need to see most.

Without this space, we are constantly reacting to life rather than making choices as to how we wish to live.

Along with Truth, Space is another prerequisite for attraction.

6. Success

Know why we don't get exactly what we want? Simple. We don't know exactly what we want. We have an idea of what we think we're *supposed* to want, but not a clear picture of what's really important to us.

Without the space to identify what we really want, we send out a half-baked thought to the Universe of our desires. Because the Universe acts like a mirror, reflecting the energy that we send out to it, we then get undercooked results sent back to us.

When we know the truth of who we really are and behave accordingly, we are in the place where we will attract what we really want. Like a moth to your porch light, what you really want will show up at your door. That's how attraction works. Like magic.

7. Attraction

When we attract what we really want out of life, we are very, very happy people. Makes sense, huh?

And this brings us full circle because being happy is the point of life, isn't it? When we understand and employ the incredible power of the Law of Attraction, we no longer need to worry, about <u>anything</u>.

8 Reasons For Becoming Abundant

Because You Are Worth It! And you Deserve it!

Because you know the importance of taking the time to feed and fuel your mind, just as you do your body everyday.

Because you are ready to release old patterns of limitation and lack that can all too easily creep back in because of "habitual rituals."

Because you understand the power of influence and how keeping the company of "abundant-conscious" people, is extremely beneficial.

Because you want to build a strong "internal foundation" of success, which you understand is necessary to support the "outer success of abundance."

Because you acknowledge that through playfully practicing the "Way of the Abundant," creating the things you want just gets easier and easier. You will flow with the energy of the abundance of spirit.

Because you understand that you will be accessing and applying powerful information in a variety of entertaining ways, that makes cultivating and creating the Abundant mindset,

AND most importantly ... because it works!

Abundance is your birthright.

11 Steps To A Successful Life

1. Make you intuitions your ally

How does your intuition speak to you? Do you receive information in words, feelings, a body sensation? Do you just know? Ask your intuition questions and pay attention to the answers and act on the information you receive.

2. What are you enthusiastic about?

The root of the word enthusiasm is entheos. It literally means "God Within." Just think, when you feel enthusiastic about your dreams it means that God is speaking through you and saying "yes" to your goals! The feeling of enthusiasm is one of the ways your intuition speaks to you. What makes you excited, happy, delighted? What do you look forward to each day? Do more of it!

3. Be clear about your goals

We are often quite clear about what we don't want. Spend time thinking about what you do want. What does your ideal life look like? Draw pictures or cut out scenes from magazines that illustrate the life you want to create. Write in your journal, envision. Spend time each day imagining your ideal life. Envision the details of that life. Imagine you are living it now. What are you wearing? What are you feeling? Who are the people around you? The power is within your mind and heart to bring forth the new life you desire.

4. Spend time in prayer and meditation

Answers often come to life's questions through self- reflection. Prayer and meditation are two ways we have of slowing down enough to listen to the still, quiet voice of our Higher Self. Remember that the answers don't always pop into your mind fully formed as you meditate or pray. You may find them slowly evolving into your consciousness over several days or weeks as you ask for insight.

5. Create positive "Self Talk"

Pay attention to what you tell yourself about yourself and your life. If the general tone is hopeful and positive you feel better and are more optimistic. William James said, "The greatest discovery of my generation is that human beings, by changing the inner attitudes of their minds, can change the outer aspects of their lives." It's easier to create a life you love when you give yourself affirmative messages.

6. **Practice and "Attitude of Gratitude"**

Research has shown that the happiest people are the ones who have gratitude for all that they have despite their circumstances. You don't have to postpone happiness until you have achieved all your goals. Joy is an inside job. In the Talmud it says, "In the world to come each of us will be called to account for all the good things God put on this earth which we refused to enjoy." Learn to appreciate the unfolding process of your life, not just the realization of your dreams.

7. **Take action**

People often get stuck because they can't figure out how to get from Point A to Point Z. What is one thing you could do that would be a next step? Take a class, talk to a friend, read a book on a topic of interest, learn a new skill. Take action on what feels exciting to you.

8. **Look for coincidences and synchronicities**

It has been said that coincidences are God's way of remaining anonymous. We often have serendipity occurring in our lives as a way to show us we are on the right path. As you trust your intuitive knowing you'll find these synchronicities occurring more often.

9. **Know that there will be ebbs and flows**

We often reach success through a series of ups and downs. When you are in a "down" place and feeling stuck, know that it won't last forever. Find some ways to enjoy your life despite the lull and continue to focus on what you want.

10. **Trust in divine order**

Maybe you're beginning to feel as Mother Theresa once did when she said, "I know God will not give me anything I can't handle. I just wish that He didn't trust me so much." The Universe has a perfect plan for your growth and unfolding as a human being. As you learn to be guided by your intuition you're beginning to act on this wisdom from the Universe.

11. **Forgive Yourself**

Remember to forgive yourself for past mistakes that you have made on this journey to success. Only by forgiveness can one truly move forward to their path to success.

<u>Creating An Extraordinary</u>
Holistic Healing Enterprise

So how do you create an extraordinary holistic healing practice? With client/customer service, that how. Get to know your clients well by connecting with them on a deep level of understanding.

Here are a few suggestions on how to create unsurpassed-extraordinary client/customer service:

1. Make a great first impression. Clients form an opinion about you in the first 10 seconds on meeting you, shaking hands and saying hello. So that first 10 seconds must become the focus of how to make them feel at ease and comfortable in your office/treatment room. Some ways of making your clients feel at home in your office are to greet them as they come in and pay attention to them, giving them a sense that they are both wanted and welcomed in your office.

2. Keep your office environment outside and inside clean, neat and inviting. Remember many clients will form an opinion about you and your healing practice as soon as they pull into your parking lot.

3. Keep your own appearance healthy, happy and professional looking. Your client does not want to receive healing from someone who appears unprofessional and sickly. The client want to come to someone who appears successful, healthy, happy and professional.

4. Ask your clients for feedback on how to improve your business. It makes your clients feel you valuable them and their ideas.

Offer clients discounts on products, or free admittance to classes or workshops you offer. This will go along way to create loyal clients who spread the word about your extraordinary holistic healing practice.

Eight Frequent Web Site Mistakes

People just starting out with their websites tend to make the same type of mistakes. It's truly amazing to see the same errors pop up again and again. You can pretty much tell whether this is someone's first, second, or third website.

Or whether they finally paid someone to design a nice site. I admit to the same beginner's mistakes. My first website, back in 1990 when the Internet was just beginning, was horrible. Fortunately I had friends to point out my mistakes, and to help me make changes in my web site. Also I eventually hired a professional web

designer I'm here to help you skip some of those evolutionary steps by avoiding beginner mistakes.

First Mistake: Welcome!

And Welcome to . . . Now most people will tell you this is a beginner mistake. Yes, if it's 18 inches tall and scrolling across the screen. Yes, if it's a neon color of any shade and centered on the page. · It's not a mistake if you're trying to set a very friendly tone for your website voice.

It's not a mistake if it begins a paragraph of really good copy explaining what this website is and does.

It's not a mistake if people email you and tell you they really like your website. Maybe they feel Welcome, which is how you want them to feel. They apparently felt welcome enough to dash off a quick email to you. Before we move on, let's improve on it. Drop the Hi! Drop the And. Just start with Welcome to . . . Then make sure you have a friendly, consistent tone throughout your website content. And if you're not a writer, well then hire one. As a matter of fact check out several writers, before hiring one.

Second Mistake: Background patterns

Please make it easy for me to read your website. Pretty much anything but a solid color in the background makes my eyes work harder than they have to in order to read your website content. You don't want tired eyes looking at your website.

Tired eyes inspire people to go watch TV instead of surf the net.
Tired eyes make people abandon sales. As do background patterns.

I don't care if you're selling massage services, tie-dye clothing, psychic readings, or DVD players. Use a solid color for your background, not that cutesy one that's just perfect. Black text on a white background is the easiest for people to read. Print your text in a white space surrounded with a pleasing background color and you're ahead of at least 75% of the web.

Third Mistake: This page is under construction

Come on!
If it's under construction don't put it up on the web. Don't build your website live on the Internet. The professional thing to do is to build your website on your hard drive, and when it's done, you THEN put it up.

Yes, when it's complete. That doesn't mean it has to be perfect. You can always go in and tweak it, change text here and there, get it nice and shiny. Just make sure that at the minimum each page has some website content on it before you put it up for the world to see.

But please, don't say, "Under construction!"

Fourth Mistake: The disappearing menu.

O.k. I know this is a hard concept to grasp, but people like their menus to stay the same. People want the same Main menu on every single page of your website. They don't want it to jump around. They want stability.

Not everyone notices when a link suddenly disappears, but almost all of them get a very uncomfortable feeling like, "hmmm, something is wrong here." Some of them (like myself) will actually click back and forth until they figure out what the error is.

Keep that menu the same. That doesn't mean that inside a page, you can't add a link. But that big menu you have at the left, top, or right must stay the same.

That means FAQ doesn't disappear when you're on the FAQ page. · It's still there just in case someone forgets they're on the FAQ page and wants to click on it again. · It's still there so that there is not a visual shift in the design of the page. · It's still there so that nothing, such as movement, pulls your customers away from the incredible website content they are reading.

Fifth Mistake: Free Website Hosting

Fine if it's a personal website. Big No-No if you're actually trying to sell something on the Internet, including your professional holistic services. Website hosting runs about $100/year, sometimes much less, and you can buy your very own domain for less than $10/year.

Sixth Mistake: E-mail addresses

Please, people! Stick to one email address.

Do not have more than one email address, it confuses customers/clients. Website hosting comes with at least one free email address if not many, many more.

Use only one! It only takes one to establish you as a professional.

One email address is all you need.

Seventh Mistake: Links.

Putting up links that relate directly to your product or service. Go beyond the box, reach outside your product line or the services you offer. Add links that contribute to your expanding market of clients or customers.

Eighth Mistake: Personal Pictures

As for pictures, yes, put one up of you. But make sure it's a professional one. And absolutely no one wants to see pictures of your cats, dogs, pets etc. Keep your pictures professional and business oriented.

Five Ways To Make Money With Your Web Site

Today, the Web is an intensely commercial medium, offering plenty of ways to make money.

Sell products and services from your site. These days, commerce is king on the Web, as everyone scrambles to enable e-commerce on their Web sites. Despite the competition, online merchants can rack up impressive sales. Be warned, though: doing it right is harder than it looks.

Point people to other sites. The Associates Program at Amazon.com and other online retailers may be simplest and easiest way to make money with your site. Simply point visitors to your site to a related book or other product on Amazon.com, for example, and you collect a commission on anything the user buys.

Sell your e-books. Even though you may sell the book in a hard copy, remember to sell it as an e-book as well.

Do email marketing. Remember, there is more to the Internet than just the World Wide Web. In many ways, email is an even more lucrative revenue source than the Web. You can sell ads on your email newsletter, and use targeted emails to alert customers about special deals or new products. Or services you offer.

Sell products or services offered by others on your web site for a fee or marketing arrangement. Offer products that can be drop shipped from your supplier, so there is little or no cost to you and no inventory.

5 Ways to Strengthen Your
Business Writing

All businesses produce written communications. From advertisements to flyers.

Here are five easy ways to make sure your writing is stunning on paper!

What Audience Are You Writing To?

Before putting pen to paper the first question to ask is "Who am I writing to, who is my audience?" Is it an advertisement aimed for a specific niche in your overall target audience? Is it a press release headed to the media?

All of these audiences process information differently, so your communications must be specifically designed to speak to these audiences. Prospective clients want to know the benefits of your services or product, while the media wants to know why it's newsworthy. Not all audiences are the same. Don't write to them in the same way.

What Is Your Main Message?

What it is that you want your audience to know? Often, many business communications, from advertisements to flyers, don't have a single, main message that the communication is built around. Before you write, do a little brainstorming and make a list: What is the one main idea of what you want to tell your audience? What is the one thing you want them exactly to understand? If you were to ask a client what's the one thing they remember from your flyer or ad, what would you like them to say?

Organize Your Points: Tell a Story

Of course, there is much more to your communications than just the one thing. These are " points." Ideally, they should support the main message. Think of it as "telling a story." It will make your message text easier for your audience to understand. Everyone likes a good story.

Avoid the "jargon trap".

Every industry (including the Holistic Healthcare) has its own specific language, from acronyms to technical terms. The list of such language, known as "jargon", is endless. And because jargon is such a part of the everyday language inside any industry, it's very easy to fall into the "jargon" trap. A good rule of thumb to follow is to think of your audience. If 95% of them are not directly involved in your industry on a professional basis, don't use the jargon.

Proofread! And Proofread!

In my time as an intuitive business counselor, I lost count to the number of times I received, letters, brochures, signs, press releases, newsletters, and any other types of communications that were full of the following: typos, bad grammar, and overall poor English. The best way to avoid this?

Have someone who have never laid eyes on the written project proofread it. Fresh eyes always spot things that writers miss. Take advantage of this phenomenon.

Holistic Green?

Holistic and Green are they compatible? YES!

As a member of the holistic healing community, I naturally have a concern for the health of people and our planet.

Since the planet- Earth that we live on is so important to our health and survival as a species. I believe our very work as healers, makes us more aware of the world around and the dangers of climate changes.

We as healers need to step forward and lead the way in being examples of lightening our impact on the planet.

This starts with us "healers" becoming a "Green Business Leader" by greening our business.

So how do I do that you ask? Well lets start with a tour of your office space, walk in the front door, is it weather-stripped, to keep our the cold and the warm air in? When you turn on the lights, what kind of bulbs are you using?

For a small investment, you can install low-watt energy saving light bulbs.

Now lets move to the bathroom. Are your paper products recycled? Do you use cloth towels instead of paper? What about your hand soap? Is it organic non toxic? And what about low-flow devices at your sink, shower and toilet?

So how do you keep your office clean? Do you use non-chemical cleaning products? If not start replacing your supplies with eco-friendly cleaners.

Ok now what you ask? Well how about your marketing material; business cards, brochures, flyers, intake forms, etc? Are they printed on recycled paper?

Also the greatest impact you can have is to move your marketing material to your web site, and when you hand out material always refer people to your web site for more information.

What's next, well I suggest green plants, they filter the air, and provide a calming effect, recycle your waste paper, cans and bottles.

Once you have done these changes, you can consider these larger investments to helping the planet be more balanced.

Soar cells, solar water heating, radiant floor heating, environmental landscaping.

Well that about it, first set your intentions them make the changes necessary to create a greened environment in your business.

Increasing Your Intuition

The rapid and increasingly unpredictable change that already characterizes the twenty-first century will require associations to move beyond database management to a culture that pursues informed intuition," write Glenn Tecker, Kermit Eide, and Jean Frankel on the opening page of their groundbreaking 1997 book, Building a Knowledge-Based Culture: Using Twenty-first Century Work and Decision-Making Systems in Associations. "...When intelligently considered, defensible information is carefully blended with expert and user instincts about the future, and when this combination is consistently expected to be used in making decisions, the organization is operating with informed intuition." More broadly, intuition is the act or faculty of knowing immediately, directly, and holistically without the use of reasoning and without being aware of how we know. For centuries it has been referred to as our "sixth sense." We talk about intuition frequently without realizing it, using words such as "gut feeling" or "instinct." We might say, "That feels right;" "I just knew it;" "It suddenly hit me;" "Something clicked into place;" or "The solution suddenly became clear."

Like a growing number of other business industry observers, Tecker and his colleagues reflect the increasingly common belief that the benefits of applied, informed intuition mean it can no longer be considered "hocus-pocus" in the management arena - far from it, in fact. In a recent interview with Executive Update, branding guru Scott Bedbury acknowledges, "I've come to the conclusion that building a brand has more to do with art, more to do with the intangible aspects of running a company, than it does with the science or the tangible processes like finances or production or supply chain operations.

It's a pretty heavy thing to say, but I do believe it. ... That's my problem with business books; they come out of the pre-quantification side. If you do that often

enough, you forget what an idea feels like. The best ideas are felt, not measured." Bedbury recalls the story of a leader at a major company who had climbed the ranks through the financial side of the business but was very ineffective as a chief officer. "A writer for Business Week summed it up simply by saying, 'He knew the math in how to run the business, but he didn't know the music in how to build a brand.' To me, that's the heart of the matter. It's both [intuition and business acumen]. It's not either/or."

And Bedbury is not just referring to work-related "hunches." A well-developed sense of intuition helps you gain clarity of vision in such areas as personal relationships, emotions, and desires. "Most people think of themselves as intuitively blocked," writes Rosemary Ellen Guiley in her book, Breakthrough Intuition: How to Achieve a Life of Abundance by Listening to the Voice Within. "They unwittingly shut themselves off from a tremendous source of guidance, wisdom, insight, creativity, and healing. ... When we allow our intuition to work for us, we are better equipped to make good decisions, for everything from driving a particular route to making career changes to investing our money to involvements with other people." We all have intuition.

It is an ability we are born with, and it occurs naturally. Just as some of us are born with innate sports or artistic abilities, some of us have easier access to our intuition. Just as we can all improve skills such as golf, so can we practice to improve our intuitive accuracy? The edge that intuitive access gives us can be learned through strategic intuition training or consultations.

According to William Bradley, CEO of W. J. Bradley Company, who has worked with intuition consultants, "My intuition has become an invaluable tool in altering the direction of my company. I have learned to use intuition with a strong dose of faith. As I am becoming more confident, I am moving from faith to trust." Barbara Feeney, a district sales leader for Doncaster, has participated not only in intuitive consultations but also in intuition trainings. She adds, "By using intuitive tools this last year, I have gone from the bottom of the barrel - number 65 out of 67 managers - to number two in the nation.

When I use my intuition in balance with my logic, days seem to flow effortlessly. When I get out of balance by being too analytical, I encounter obstacles and problems that seem to crop up out of nowhere." With increased confidence in their inner voice, people often see improvement in personal and professional relationships, teamwork, planning, sales, and other areas. We are better able to focus, see more options, broaden our awareness, and improve results.

The Four Phases of Intuition
Accessing your intuition can become second nature when you become more aware of the four phases of the intuitive process.

Preparation
The first phase involves preparation and analysis, and you can easily get stuck here. You use your analytical mind to gather facts and learn about a particular issue or situation. You may keep looking for answers because you feel they are somehow buried in the facts and data.

Incubation
The second phase requires you to let go of the facts for a while and permit your analytical mind to rest. This is vitally important in accessing intuition. You might meditate, take a walk, engage in a favorite sport or pastime, listen to soothing music, or consciously turn your attention to another subject. It is from this state of being open to receiving the answer, rather than pursuing the answer, that your intuitive flash or insight can spring.

Insight
You may receive your intuitive insights through a variety of modes - visual images, verbal messages, physical sensations, emotional feelings, or environmental cues - or you may just have an immediate general sense of knowing. One mode of reception is just as valuable as another, and the messages you receive may have meaning only for you. With practice, you may receive insights through other modes as well. For example, you may unexpectedly read a sentence in a book or hear a song that answers a question. You may have a sudden gut feeling or an emotional response to a topic. You may receive an unexpected phone call or feel an immediate overall sense of knowing while in the shower.

Validation
Once you receive the insight, you take time again to use your analytical mind and interpret the results. You check to see if the message you received fully solves the problem or answers the question at hand. The process of verifying can be immediate or may continue through time. If you think an intuitive flash is inconclusive, you can return to the beginning of the process with increased knowledge. You simply ask yourself for another insight to verify or clarify the previous message. In the process of preparing, incubating, receiving, and verifying your insights, you sometimes find that your intuitive faculty is blocked, thereby muddying or distorting your vision.

Your mind can be clouded by intrusive thoughts, emotions, or someone else's influence. Mental stress can be a major component in blocking your intuitive wisdom. Conscious or unconscious fear also can block you from proceeding through the phases of the intuitive process. Fear keeps you from beginning the process, relaxing fully, and receiving intuitive knowledge. It distorts your interpretation and interrupts implementation of the results. Finally, negative thinking, as well as wishful thinking, can contaminate your acknowledgment and interpretation. States of mind such as anger, anxiety, fatigue, and depression also can interfere with your awareness of intuitive signals and can pollute your interpretations.

Increasing Your Intuition

Most important in further developing your intuition is the belief that we all have intuition as an innate ability. That belief allows you to best access your intuition. You also must trust that your insights can be valid; this enables you to properly interpret your intuitive flashes. Last, you learn how to minimize the blocks to intuition.

Here are some techniques we use to help people navigate the four phases of intuition.

Grounding the Body

This plants your feet firmly on the ground. It allows you to release stress, relax, and be more present with your environment. By becoming "grounded," you open yourself to the intuitive process. Martial arts experts employ similar grounding techniques. You can become grounded in different ways. You can go camping, sit in the grass, or relax by the ocean. These methods involve being in a natural environment. The problem is that, due to busy schedules, most of us do not have the opportunity to spend an extended amount of time in nature during our day. If that's the case, try this simple technique to ground yourself at home or work. First, sit with your feet on the floor. Relax and let your eyes close. Next, with your imagination, send a cord from the base of your spine down to the center of the Earth. Imagine a ship releasing an anchor to the ocean floor. Just as this stabilizes a ship in the storm, so does your grounding cord keep you centered through a stress-filled day? Once you are attached from the base of your spine to the center of the Earth, you can use your grounding cord as a conduit that releases stress. Simply command stress or any irritation to fall down the grounding cord; then imagine filling the cleared spaces with bright sunlight, a nourishing element for your body.

Clearing the Mind

Your head often can be filled with mind clutter that can make you feel slightly off-center. By clearing away mental distractions, you can improve your internal vision. You can do this by imagining that you are opening a pathway through your ears, turning on a fan, and blowing out the mind chatter. You then can fill this cleared space with your own pure thoughts. Visualize this as water pouring into your head from a shower spigot. Only when your mind is clear can you receive uncontaminated intuitions.

Owning your Space

Here you give yourself some room. You establish a boundary around yourself like a fence around a valuable piece of property.

You try to keep that property as clear as possible. Respecting Others You allow others to have boundaries as well. By respecting the spaces surrounding others, you are better able to maintain your own space.

By neither invading nor being invaded, you can relax and focus on the intuitive process. Also wearing an auraurolite pendant to absorb negative energy can protect your space.

Learning these and other techniques - through related reading, personal intuitive consultations, or group intuition trainings can immediately affect your personal and professional life.

Intuitive tools can help you make decisions more easily and with more confidence. By being grounded, you can be more present and in touch with the issues. By clearing your mind, you can see more clearly and hear yourself think. By owning your own space and respecting that of others, you can let go of stress, relax, and communicate with the people around you.

A life aided by well-developed intuition can help ensure that you stay on your own unique path to self-fulfillment and happiness.

Using Intuition in your business process

There are 4 primary ways you receive intuitive information:

- **Emotions**: Intuitive information often comes through your feelings or emotions. You may simply "feel right" about your decision to hire that new business consultant. Or conversely you might experience an unexplained sense of distrust despite this individual's great credentials.

- **Physical :** The Japanese call using intuition "stomach art." We call such sensations a "gut feeling." You've just been offered the "perfect job" and yet you notice that when you think about accepting the position your body feels heavy or there's a knot in your stomach. My client Jane reported she felt this way after receiving a recent job offer. She couldn't shake the impression that something was "not right" with the company. She described feeling physically uncomfortable when she thought of joining the firm. Despite her reservations, she accepted the position because she couldn't think of any logical reason to turn it down. The company went bankrupt within three months after she started.

- **Thoughts**: You may receive a sudden flash of understanding. This is sometimes called the "Eureka" effect.

- **Assessing Intuitive Data:** You have to make a choice. You've done due diligence. You've researched, asked questions and have all the facts in front of you. You still don't know what decision to make. The next step you take requires intuitive input.

Here are four questions to stimulate the guidance from your intuition.

1. **What am I ready to act on right now?** Your decision may require a small step, not a huge leap. Quite often when you take a step forward more information becomes available to you. Many people report that as they make an intuitive choice towards what proves to be a correct decision, events begin flowing more easily and effortlessly. Doors to opportunity open and synchronicity and coincidence begin to occur.

2. **Which of my choices has the most "vitality?"** Think of the options you have before you. Which one are you drawn to? Is there one that leaps to your attention and captures your interest? You may experience a visceral charge about pursuing this course of action. Remember that kinesthetic or physical sensations are one of the ways that intuition communicates.

3. **How do I feel about my choices?** Do you feel excited or passionate about one more than the others? This is one of the ways that intuition will point to the direction you should follow. Conversely, if a choice makes you feel depressed or discouraged, or you feel a great deal of resistance, you're ignoring a strong intuitive message if you continue on this path.

4. **What do I think about this decision?** Many people have great success receiving intuitive information through writing. This technique is similar to brainstorming. Write a series of questions about your choices. Make the time to routinely check in with your intuition and you will be rewarded with faster, stronger and more accurate insight. The benefit? You'll gain a competitive advantage that will help you become a better player in the new economy.

<u>Attracting Clientele</u>

Building a successful business is easy if one is honest, sincere and has integrity.

For most holistic healers it can be difficult to face the challenge of marketing yourself and building a clientele. This challenge can be enhanced by the desire not to commercialize holistic healing in compromise of your spiritual values.

A potential barrier to success that many holistic healers face in marketing themselves is the balance between the desire to give and the practicalities of living in an economically driven world. Often, a fear of receiving money for doing holistic healing interferes with the ability to build a thriving practice.

Earning money is not a bad thing - but possessing a belief that it is can sabotage your success in building a successful practice. One way to address this is to realize that what we get paid for our services as a holistic healer is an exchange of energy that recognizes the value of your healing knowledge and treatment process. By viewing money as a method of exchange that provides balance between client and healer we become more comfortable with our self worth and receiving financial abundance.

The techniques used in building any business can be used by the holistic practitioner, perhaps with a few minor adjustments and focusing on the intention behind them. The holistic healer must be clear in their mind that the purpose behind using marketing tools is to share their knowledge of holistic healing and living with the community, and then a successful relationship with clients can be reached.

One of the basic techniques for building any business is getting to know your clients. As a holistic healer your clients are those who come to you to receive the benefits of healing.

Get to know the names of your clients, and some history about them. Also networking with other holistic professionals, community groups, professional organizations and such, improves your standing in the community and spreads the word about your valuable healing practice.

Greeting your clients each time by shaking hands, when you see them personalizes them, and it gives you the opportunity to tune into their physical presence. As you physically connect with your clients you create a one-on-one bond that depends the client healer relationship.

Just as important as it is to greet your clients, it is equally important to make yourself available to answer their questions about the healing treatments, protocols, procedures, etc.

Two Final Techniques

1. An honest assessment of how much time and energy you are wiling to spend on networking, teaching classes, workshops or lecturing, and cultivating a clientele.

Burn-out and boredom are energy zappers that can sneak up on you and rob you of your passion for healing. By remaining present while doing healings you avoid the healing from becoming routine, you keep yourself fresh and alive. If you find yourself not being present or going through the motions as a routine, it may be time for a little quiet reflection as to where your healing practice is going.

2. Another technique for fostering greater self-awareness is committing to your own personal education. How often do you take seminars, classes or workshops? Being inspired by another healer can help to further your own healing abilities. Taking a workshop, class can refresh your spirit as well as avail you of new healing techniques to apply in your own healing practice/business. As you stay fresh your staff and clients perceive that energy and will recommit to their jobs and their healing journey.

As you try some of these techniques for yourself, you will see which ones work well for you and match with your personality, and personal goals as a holistic healer. Trust your intuition as you connect with your clients on a deeper level and watch as they become more committed to their own healing journey. And in the process of healing your clients on this journey, watch your business/practice grow and prosper.

The Spiritual Path Of Operating a Holistic Business

Of all the paths I have followed in my life, operating a healing center,(The Family of Light Healing & Yoga Centre) has been the most challenging and rewarding. Every day that I work for myself is a day I come face to face with my worldview and my belief system. Working for myself is a constant reminder that my success is determined more by my state of mind than by external events.

Here are a few practical implications of operating your holistic business as spiritual path. In my experience, these implications hold true regardless of your religious beliefs.

1) I am responsible for the value of my work and for how it is perceived in the world. The value that my clients place on my work is not likely to exceed the value I place on it.

2) Prosperity is directly related to my priorities. It is up to me to be clear about what prosperity means for me and to make these things a priority.

3) Prosperity is also directly related to my expectations. When I expect the best, I make the most of each opportunity, including the opportunities disguised as disappointments.

4) My experience of success and failure is directly related to my fundamental expectations about life. If I believe that things generally go wrong, they will.

5) Marketing is an inside job. When I know what I do, love what I do, and am willing to share what I do, marketing is natural, effortless, and sustainable.

6) The best attitude in the world is insufficient without action. I get results when I walk my talk.

7) When I am doing my right work I bless everyone around me. The more on purpose and prosperous I am, the more those blessings seed purpose and prosperity for others.

8) When I laugh at and learn from my mistakes I profit from adversity.

9) When I am clear that my business is a gift and when I trust that more will be given, I surf the shifting tides of success with grace and good humor.

10) When I'm willing to know what I want and to ask for it, I am likely to get it (or something of greater value).

11) Networking with likeminded professional creates a space for sharing ideas & love of yourself.

12) Remember to operate your business like it's part of the family, it needs love & attention just like other family members do.

Afterthoughts

The handbook is meant to be used as a guide on the journey of operating a holistic enterprise.

I have used the tips, ideas, suggestions and processes used in this handbook.
And for 30 years have operated several successful businesses both retail and service businesses.

It is my hope that this handbook along with the workshop that I teach these principles will allow the holistic practitioner/business owner to succeed.

With passion, intuition and knowledge one can operate a financially successful holistic enterprise.

This handbook has been many years in the making and is a collection of thoughts, ideas and knowledge I have gained along the way operating a mobile Healing centre. The joy of this endeavor has made my life one of great adventure and I feel so very blessed to be of service to the world in bring about the transformation of change that is occurring at this time on the planet.

I would appreciate any feedback on this handbook that those of you who use this in your handbook choose to share.

Blessing to all who use this handbook,
                            Charles Lightwalker

<u>Holistic Business Books</u>

The Soul of Money   Lynne Twist

The Seven Laws of Money   M. Phillips

The Secrets of Word of Mouth Marketing   George Silverman

101 Ways to Boost Your web Traffic Thomas Wong

How To Be Your Own Publicist   Jessica Hatchigan

Cracking the Millionaire Code   Hansen & Allen

Ask and It Is Given   E & J Hicks

Visionary Business   Marc Allen

The Spiritual Millionaire   Keith C. Smith

The Fine Art of Small Talk   Debra Fine

Business Know-How Janet Attard

Creating Customer Evangelists   McConnell & Huba

The Anatomy of Buzz Emanuel Rosen

The Instant Millionaire   Mark Fisher

Dating Your Money   Jennifer S. Wilkov

Simple Living Investments   Michael Phillips

The Self Publishing Manual Dan Poynter

101 Ways to Promote Your Web Site Susan Sweeney

The Power of Concentration Theron Q. Dumont

Gorilla Web Site Marketing Glenn Canady

The Creating Game   Linda Bretherton

Marketing for the Holistic Practitioner   Michelle A. Vandepas

The Abundance book   Lawarence Crane

The Sedona Method Hale Dwoskin

<u>Other Books by Charles</u>

Crystaline Reiki Book   **$19.00**
Sound Healing with Tuning Forks
Advanced Sound Healing with Tuning Forks
Quantum Healing: the Synergy of Chiropractic and Reiki
Medical Intuition Handbook
Medical Intuition and Muscle Testing
Crystal Reiki Workbook
Whip Flash Soup: Poetry
Crystal and Gemstone Healing Course Book
Vibrational Yoga

<u>Class schedule</u>

Operating a Holistic Enterprise

Introductions: Everyone introduce themselves, 5 minutes for each person to tell a little bit about themselves, why they are here, etc.

Centering Meditation

Set the Intention: Have each participant set their intentions for their business, goals, ideas objectives, etc.

Lecture: **Starting a Practice/Business**
Brief overview of starting a business and the process involved.

Exercise: <u>Write a business description</u>
This should be a short description of yourself and what you intend to do.
Don't be afraid to write down everything.

- Who you are (background)
- Why are you starting this business
- Where will the business be located
- How will you promote the business

Have classmates read their brief description to class to get feedback, input and ideas on how to rewrite this description. Have students rewrite their description as a homework assignment.

Class break 15 minutes Bathroom use, stretching, etc.

Question: Does Your Business Plan contain?

- Business Description
- Market Research
- Promotion
- Cash Flow Explanations

- Cash Flow Projections
- Profit and Loss Charts (12 months-36 months)

Business Materials Needed:

- Business Cards
- Brochures
- Educational Material
- Flyers
- Products Displays
- Hours of Operation
- Fee Schedule

Business Materials Optional

- Appointment cards
- Scheduling book
- Post office box

Class break 15 minutes Bathroom use, stretching, etc.

9 781835 381984